HOW TO MAKE BR

CW00501451

Simplified Guide For Beginners On Bracelets Making For Various Purposes, Techniques, Patterns And Procedures To Troubleshooting Common Mistakes

CHARLES ELSIE

CHAPTER ONE

Introduction To Making Bracelets: A Creative Journey

Making bracelets is a fun and adaptable pastime that has been loved for ages. It offers a medium for individual expression, enabling you to craft stunning wearable artworks that capture your sense of fashion, character, and inventiveness. Whether you are an expert jewelry maker or a total novice, making bracelets may be a fulfilling and enjoyable hobby.

From a Historical Angle:

The art of crafting bracelets has a long history in human history. Archaeological discoveries have shown proof of bracelets from thousands of years ago, fashioned from a variety of materials such as metals, stones, shells, and bones. These early works of art represented cultural customs, social standing, and individual beliefs while also serving ornamental and symbolic functions.

Bracelets have had a variety of symbolic connotations throughout history. They have been worn as religious emblems, love and friendship gifts, and protective talismans. Bracelets are significant gifts and personal statements since they still express messages and feelings in modern times.

Contemporary Appeal:

Making bracelets has become a popular art form in the modern day, as enthusiasts and professionals alike experiment with a wide range of materials, methods, and designs. Regardless of your interests in wire wrapping, beadwork, macramé, or metalworking, there is a bracelet-making technique that will work for you and your abilities.

Why Make Your Bracelets?

1. Creative outlet: Designing and creating wearable artwork is made possible by the very creative process of making bracelets. You can freely play around with hues, textures, and patterns to make one-of-a-kind jewelry that complements your style.

2. Customization: You have total control over the design when you create your bracelets, so you can make sure that every item expresses your individuality and flawlessly matches your outfit. Additionally, bracelets can be customized to provide unique and heartfelt gifts for loved ones.

Three. Meditative and soothing: Making bracelets can be a soothing and therapeutic hobby.

Crafts that include rhythms, like bead stringing, knotting, or metal sculpting, can reduce stress and promote relaxation.

4. Cost-Effectiveness: Creating your bracelets is a reasonably priced method to get fine,

handcrafted jewelry. You may create gorgeous things that would normally cost a lot of money in stores by choosing materials that suit your budget.

5. Skill Development: The ability to make bracelets may be honed with practice.

As you experiment with new methods and materials, you'll hone your workmanship and pick up useful jewelry-making abilities.

6. Socialization: Making bracelets together can be a fun hobby. To discuss concepts, methods, and inspiration, get together with friends or join online crafting communities. It's a great opportunity to meet people who are as passionate about jewelry manufacturing as you are.

<u>Starting Point:</u>

It's important to acquire the required supplies, equipment, and resources before starting your bracelet-making project. This could contain pliers, wires, clasps, beads, threads, and tutorials or instruction manuals, depending on the technique you have chosen. You will find that there are countless options as you explore the realm of bracelet-making, and the only thing stopping you from creating something amazing is your creativity.

We will examine a range of bracelet-making methods in this thorough tutorial, from simple stringing and knotting to intricate wirework and metal fabrication. You will find detailed directions, advice, and imaginative ideas in every chapter to help you become an expert bracelet maker and let your creativity run wild. Making bracelets is a gratifying and captivating activity that opens up a world of creative possibilities, whether you're doing it for yourself or to share your creations with others.

Now, let's embark on this fascinating journey of creating story-telling bracelets to adorn wrists!

A Brief History Of Bracelets

For thousands of years, people have adorned their wrists with bracelets, which are timeless and multipurpose pieces of jewelry.

Its broad and varied history reflects the aesthetic, social, and cultural advancements of many civilizations across time. A fascinating trip through human inventiveness and evolution, the history of bracelets has evolved from humble beginnings to signifying prestige, love, and fashion.

First. Ancient Origins: The history of bracelets extends back to the time of ancient civilizations. Indeed, some of the oldest known bracelets date back to 5000 BCE and were found in Mesopotamia and Egypt.

Materials such as shells, wood, and bone were used to make these ancient bracelets. Some bracelets are thought to have been worn as protection charms, and they had both practical and ornamental functions.

2. Symbolism in Ancient Cultures: In many ancient communities, bracelets were deeply symbolic of both culture and religion.

During the ancient Egyptian era, bracelets served as both a status and riches symbol and an amulet to ward off evil spirits. Bracelets were frequently offered as expressions of friendship and affection in classical Greece and Rome.

Three. Medieval and Renaissance Eras: Bracelets started to take on increasingly complex shapes during this time. The nobles and aristocracy started wearing bracelets made of gold and silver that were set with gemstones. Jewelry design was influenced by the Renaissance's resurgence of interest in classical art and culture.

Ancient civilizations served as inspiration for the elaborate designs and motifs used in bracelet design.

4. In the 19th century, there was a rebirth of interest in sentimental jewelry during the Victorian era, and bracelets were a major part of

this trend. During this period, charm bracelets, mourning bracelets, and lockets gained popularity. These bracelets served as mementos and tokens of affection, frequently holding small photographs or strands of hair.

5. The Art Nouveau Movement: Known for its flowing, organic designs, the Art Nouveau movement took place in the late 19th and early 20th centuries. These were the years when semi-precious gemstones, glass, enamel, and other materials were frequently used to create elaborate, nature-inspired bracelet designs. Beautiful Art Nouveau bracelets were made by famed jewelry designer René Lalique at this time.

6. The Roaring Twenties: The 1920s were a time of social emancipation and transformation, which was represented in the jewelry and clothing of the day. The practice of stacking several bangles on one arm to create a dramatic and stylish appearance was made popular by flapper females. A larger range of people were able to

purchase bracelets thanks to the use of materials like bakelite and costume jewelry.

6. Modern & Contemporary Bracelets: Classic bracelet designs like the Love Bracelet and the Juste un Clou bracelet were first introduced by renowned jewelry designers like Cartier in the middle of the 20th century.

These pieces paired contemporary, minimalist design with high-end materials. A renewed trend in the 21st century has been personalized and meaningful wristbands, which are frequently engraved with names, dates, or inspirational sayings.

8. Bracelets still have cultural and personal relevance today, owing to their symbolism.

To commemorate important events like birthdays, marriages, and anniversaries, they are frequently given and received as gifts.

Many people wear bracelets, such as religious, friendship, or awareness bracelets, as a representation of their identities, affiliations, or beliefs.

In 9. Sustainable & Ethical Jewelry: The ethical and environmental effects of jewelry creation have come to light in recent years. As a result, materials for bracelets made from ethical and ecological sources—like recycled metals and fair-trade gemstones—are becoming more and more popular.

the evolution of bracelets bears witness to the universal human need for symbolism, decoration, and expression. Bracelets have undergone significant design and meaning changes over time, yet they have remained a vital component of human culture and self-expression since their modest beginnings in ancient civilizations and ongoing appeal in the present era.

Benefits Of Making Bracelets

A fun and fulfilling activity, bracelet-making has many advantages, from creativity and self-satisfaction to relaxation and even financial gain. The benefits are vast, regardless of whether you make bracelets as a hobby or are thinking about making it into a small business. We'll look at the many advantages of bracelet creation here.

1. Self-expression and creativity: Making bracelets enables you to express your inner artist. Through your crafts, you may show your style and personality by experimenting with different colors, patterns, materials, and designs.

2. Stress Reduction: Crafting, such as bracelet-making, can be a healing activity. Bead stringing and weaving are examples of repetitive, rhythmic activities that can ease anxiety and tension and encourage relaxation.

3. Focus and Mindfulness: Making bracelets calls for focus and meticulous attention to detail. This can help you become more conscious as you lose yourself in the creative process and put anxieties and concerns aside.

4. Emotion of Success: Finishing a jewelry project makes you feel accomplished. Having a concrete, finished product that you created yourself can increase confidence and self-worth.

5. Customized Gifts: Bracelets crafted by hand are heartfelt and individualized presents for loved ones.

Making the gift even more personal is the option to customize the design to the recipient's tastes.

6. Social Interaction: Crafting bracelets can be a group endeavor. Participating in classes or joining crafts clubs offers chances to engage with like-minded people, exchange ideas, and form social bonds.

6. Enhanced Fine Motor abilities: The dexterous effort required to make bracelets contributes to the improvement of fine motor abilities. Children can benefit most from this as it improves their dexterity and hand-eye coordination.

8. Cost-effectiveness: If you enjoy crafting and gathering ingredients over time, creating your bracelets may prove to be more affordable than purchasing them. With the same amount of money as purchasing a single bracelet, you can make several pieces.

In 9. Eco-Friendly: Making your bracelets lets you select sustainable and eco-friendly materials, which lessens the impact you have on the environment. You can recycle materials for your designs or reuse antique jewelry.

10. Profit Potential: You can make a small business out of your hobby of producing bracelets if you're very talented and driven. You may make extra money or perhaps turn your artistic endeavors into a full-time job by selling them online or at neighborhood markets.

11. Customization: The design is entirely up to you when you create your bracelets. You can design pieces that go well with your ensembles,

express your emotions, or are appropriate for particular events.

12. Mental Stimulation: Doing creative things, such as crafting bracelets, helps to stimulate your mind. It keeps your mind sharp and flexible by promoting problem-solving, pattern identification, and the acquisition of new abilities.

13. Personal Development: Learning and development are fostered by the hobby of bracelet creation. Your understanding of jewelry creation methods, supplies, and trends may always be increased.

14. Relax and Disconnect: Making bracelets is a great way to get away from screens and engage in a hands-on, analog pastime in a world full of digital distractions.

15. Creative Satisfaction: Crafting exquisite bracelets is an artistic endeavor. The fulfillment that arises from creating wearable art that is both visually beautiful and useful is profound.

creating bracelets has advantages that go well beyond the final item. Personal development, leisure, social interaction, and the possibility of financial gain are all provided by this artistic pastime.

Making bracelets is a rewarding and pleasurable hobby, regardless of whether you plan to share your creations with the world or keep them for yourself.

Getting Started

Starting a bracelet-making business can be a fulfilling and imaginative pastime. This tutorial will assist you in beginning your adventure of creating bracelets, whether your goal is to create leather cuffs, beaded jewelry, or friendship bracelets.

First. Select the Style of Bracelet:

It's important to choose the type of bracelet you want to make before actually starting. Here are a few well-liked choices to think about:

- Friendship Bracelets: These have different knotting techniques and are usually created with colorful threads. They're ideal for novices and also make wonderful presents.

- Beaded Bracelets: Beaded bracelets use a variety of beads, including wood, glass, and gemstones, in varying sizes. Basic jewelry-making and stringing abilities are required.

- Macramé Bracelets: This art form entails the careful knotting of strands to form beautiful patterns. To get good at this method, you'll need to practice and have some patience.

- Wire-Wrapped Bracelets: These bracelets have distinctive designs thanks to the wire that's used to wrap and hold stones or beads.

For this technique, some prior wire work experience is beneficial.

• Leather Bracelets: Using a variety of leatherworking techniques, such as stitching, braiding, and tooling, leather bracelets can be made in an intricate or simple design.

2. Assemble Materials:

After deciding on the style of bracelet you want, gather the required materials. Here's a broad overview to get you going:

For Bracelets of Friendship:

- Craft or embroidery thread in the colors of your choice
- Shears.
- Tape or a clipboard to keep your work in place
- Optional closures such as clasps or buttons

For Bracelets with Beads:

Beads of your preference

- Stretch cord or beading wire

Conclusions or shutdowns

• Pliers and beading needles (for more complex designs)

In regards to Macramé Bracelets:

• Harness twine or macramé cord

• Shears.

• A clipboard or tape to keep your work in place

• Charms or beads are optional for extra adornment.

For Bracelets Wrapped with Wire:

• Wire (colored gold, silver, or copper)

• Stones or beads

• Flat-nose pliers, round-nose pliers, and wire cutters

Conclusions or shutdowns

Concerning Leather Bracelets:

• Cords or strips of leather

• equipment for working with leather (punching, cutting, and sewing equipment)

- Fastenings such as buckles or snaps
- Leather dye and finish are optional.

Three. Learn the Fundamentals:

Every bracelet style uses a different set of techniques. Practice the fundamentals first until you feel comfortable:

- Friendship Bracelets: Acquire knowledge of basic knotting methods, such as the diagonal, forward, and reverse knots. Play around with various designs and color schemes.
- Beaded Bracelets: Learn how to string beads, crimp beads, and make basic jewelry closures.
- Macramé Bracelets: Start by learning how to tie simple knots like the half-hitch and square knot. Create patterns by experimenting with different knot combinations.
- Wire-wrapped bracelets: Discover how to secure beads or stones with wire loops, wraps, and spirals.

• Leather Bracelets: Learn how to cut, sew, and braid leather. Play around with finishing and tooling to add patterns and texture.

4. Look for Inspiration

Look through websites, crafting books, and social media sites like Pinterest and Instagram to get ideas and how-tos for bracelet designs. Participating in online bracelet-making communities or forums can facilitate communication with other aficionados and provide you with helpful advice.

5. Execution and Trial:

Making bracelets is a craft that gets better with practice. As your talents advance, start with simpler tasks and work your way up to more intricate designs. Don't be scared to play around with fabrics, colors, and patterns to create one-of-a-kind pieces that express your flair.

6. Safety Measures:

Prioritize safety above everything else when handling crafting supplies. In case you're working with chemicals or adhesives, make sure you wear protective gear, work in an area with adequate ventilation, and use the right tools.

Keep in mind that creating bracelets is a flexible and entertaining pastime that can give you a feeling of creative release and success. Beginning to make bracelets may be a fun path of self-expression and craftsmanship, regardless of whether you make them for yourself, as gifts, or even as a possible business venture.

CHAPTER TWO

Bracelet Making Materials

A well-liked and artistic hobby that enables people to show their individuality and make one-of-a-kind jewelry is bracelet crafting.

The ultimate style, longevity, and quality of the bracelet are greatly influenced by the materials used in its construction. Many different materials may be used to make bracelets, and each has unique qualities and visual appeal.

We will go into the realm of bracelet-making materials in this in-depth examination, going through the most popular choices, their characteristics, and how well they work with various bracelet types.

1. Charms:

- Seed Beads: These tiny beads are perfect for complex designs and delicate beadwork.

They are available in a variety of hues.

• Glass beads: Glass beads may give your bracelet designs a touch of glitz and refinement. They come in a variety of sizes, shapes, and finishes.

• Gemstone Beads: Add natural beauty and mystical qualities to your bracelets with gemstone beads like amethyst, lapis lazuli, and turquoise.

• Wooden Beads: Ideal for bohemian or rustic bracelet styles, wooden beads are earthy and lightweight.

2. Materials for Strings:

• Elastic Cord: Stretch bracelets may be easily worn and fitted comfortably with the help of elastic cords.

• Beading wire: A robust, flexible wire coated in nylon that is ideal for crafting bracelets with clasps that have structure.

• Hemp Cord: Often used for macramé and bohemian-inspired bracelets, natural hemp cord has a rustic, organic appearance.

3. Metal Elements:

• Clasps: A bracelet must have a clasp.

There are many different types of clasps, including magnetic, toggle, and lobster clasps.

Jump rings are tiny metal rings that are used to fasten charms, beads, or other components to the bracelet's main framework.

• Spacer Beads: You may divide and add detail to your design with metal spacer beads.

4. Pendants and Charms:

• Metal charms: You can personalize these with symbols, hearts, or animals to fit the bracelet's theme or emotion.

• Charms with vivid enamel coatings: These charms give your design a whimsical and vibrant flash of color.

• Birthstone pendants: Bracelets can be made more meaningful and individualized by adding birthstone pendants.

5. Resources and Results:

• Needles: To thread beads onto stringing materials, beading needles are a necessity.

• Pliers: For handling wire and adding finishing touches, round-nose, flat-nose, and crimping pliers are useful.

• Crimps and Crimp Covers: These findings give your bracelet a finished appearance and secure the ends of the beading wire.

The use of bead mats keeps beads from rolling away as you work by providing a non-slip surface.

6. Natural Resources:

• Leather Cord: Often used in wrap- or braided-style bracelet designs, leather lends a tough and rustic appearance to bracelets.

• Cotton Thread: Available in a variety of hues, cotton thread is perfect for friendship bracelets and embroidery-style designs.

6. Blended Media:

• Resin: For a distinctive and artistic touch, include resin components such as glitter, dried flowers, or little trinkets.

• Polymer Clay: Craft unique clay beads and focal pieces that you may include in your designs after baking them to a solid state.

8. Chain and Wire:

• Wire: Crafters can make elaborate wire-wrapped decorations or structural components by using different gauges of wire.

• Chain: Various chain types, including curb, snake, and cable chains, can be the focal point or an accent in bracelet designs.

It is important to keep the overall style, concept, and intent of your design in mind when selecting materials for your bracelet design. Trying out various materials and combinations can result in the development of exquisite, one-of-a-kind bracelets that express your individuality and inventiveness. There are a plethora of materials to choose from when creating bracelets, whether your style is bohemian chic, classic elegance, or whimsical charm bracelets.

Basic Bracelet Patterns

Fundamental bracelet designs serve as the foundation for the complex and vibrant world of friendship bracelets. These straightforward patterns serve as the cornerstone for more intricate and imaginative patterns.

To create beautiful bracelets, it is necessary to grasp and become proficient with basic bracelet patterns, regardless of expertise level. We will go into the foundations of basic bracelet patterns in this in-depth investigation, including their history, materials, processes, and variants.

Friendship Bracelets' Past

Let us take a quick look at the history of friendship bracelets before we get into the fundamental bracelet patterns. The centuries-long cultural legacy of these handcrafted items is rich and varied. Although their exact origins are unknown, they have been discovered all over the world in a variety of shapes.

1. Ancient Origins: The origins of friendship bracelets can be traced to the indigenous peoples of Central and South America, who employed complex knotting techniques to fashion ornamental and symbolic jewelry. Oftentimes, these bracelets were offered as expressions of love or affection.

2. Hippie Era: During the counterculture movement of the 1960s and 1970s, friendship bracelets became increasingly popular.

Their vivid hues and straightforward patterns captivated a generation yearning for self-expression, and they transpired to become a symbol of harmony, love, and peace.

3. Global Influence: As friendship bracelets developed throughout time, they included techniques from many different civilizations, such as Native American weaving and Middle Eastern macramé. The wide variety of designs that we have now is the consequence of this blending of styles.

Supplies For Simple Bracelet Designs

A long list of supplies is not necessary to create simple bracelet patterns. Generally, you'll need the following:

1. Embroidery Floss or Thread: Typically, friendship bracelets are made with embroidery floss or thread. It comes in a broad range of hues, which opens up countless creative options.

2. scissors: To cut the floss neatly, you'll need a pair of sharp scissors.

3. Safety pins or tape: To secure your bracelet while you work on it, you'll need safety pins or tape.

Fundamental Bracelet Methods

1. Knotting: The basic method for creating friendship bracelets is knotting. Two main types of knots exist:

• Forward Knot: To tie a knot, take one thread and cross it over the other.

• Backward Knot: This is the forward knot reversed, with one thread wrapped around the other in the other direction.

2. Color Patterns: Simple color patterns are a common feature of basic bracelet patterns. When you knot together specific threads with care, you can make designs such as checkerboards, diagonals, and stripes.

3. Braiding: You can add braiding techniques to your bracelet designs in addition to knotting techniques. Compared to knotted bracelets,

braided friendship bracelets usually include more strands of thread.

Common Simple Bracelet Designs

1. Candy Stripe: One of the simplest and most identifiable patterns is the candy stripe.

It is made out of a straightforward alternating stripe design that is made by knotting two threads of different colors together.

2. Chevron: Rows of diagonal knots are repeated to produce V-shaped shapes in chevron patterns. Based on the number of rows and colors used, they can be as basic or sophisticated as you wish.

3. Diamonds: To create diamond forms, rows of diagonal knots must intersect. This is known as a diamond pattern. This design gives your bracelets a refined look.

4. Zigzag: By switching between forward and backward knots, zigzag patterns have a recurring

zigzag design. It's an aesthetically pleasing pattern that presents a little extra difficulty.

5. Spiral: The distinctive feature of spiral bracelets is their helix- or spiral-like design, which is made by interlacing threads in a particular order. When done with vivid colors, this pattern can be hypnotic.

Changes And Originality

The ease of use and adaptability of simple bracelet patterns are what make them so beautiful. After you've grasped the principles, you can express yourself freely. Try out various color combos, and knot styles, and even embellish your bracelets with beads or charms to give them a special touch. Using the "letter" or "alpha" patterns, you may even add initials, names, or messages to customize your bracelets.

To sum up, the art of creating friendship bracelets is built on the foundation of basic bracelet patterns. For both novice and seasoned crafters, familiarizing oneself with the materials, methods, history, and widely used patterns is an excellent place to start.

Crafting bracelets may be a creative way to express yourself, give meaningful gifts, or show friendship. These easy-to-follow patterns provide many creative options. Now go grab some embroidery floss and begin creating lovely and meaningful bracelets by knotting.

Step-By-Step Bracelet Making

Making bracelets is a fun and fulfilling pastime that enables you to express your creativity and make lovely, customized accessories.

Be it a novice or a seasoned jewelry maker, making bracelets by hand is a fun project that can provide one-of-a-kind wearable artwork. We'll take you step-by-step through the entire bracelet-making process in this guide, from material selection to applying finishing touches.

Step 1: Gather Your Materials

Gathering all the components is the first stage in creating a bracelet. The materials you choose will rely on your design and taste. Below is a general list of items you may require:

• Beads: You can use a range of beads, including metal, acrylic, glass, and gemstone or wood beads. Pick beads that go well with your design.

• Stringing Material: Leather cord, nylon thread, stretch cord, and beading wire are common choices. The decision is based on your desired durability and design.

The clasps on the bracelet are used to fasten it around your wrist. Magnetic clasps, toggle clasps, and lobster clasps are typical choices.

• Needles and Tools: To work with the materials, you might require pliers, wire cutters, beading needles, and crimping tools.

• Spacer beads and findings: These accent pieces give your bracelet a finished appearance and help keep it in place.

• Design Board: Before stringing, you can plan your design and arrange your beads with the aid of a design board or bead mat.

Step 2: Arrange Your Layout

Having a clear idea in mind is vital before you begin stringing beads. Take into account elements such as pattern, color palette, and bead placement. To see how your design will look in the end, you can sketch it digitally or on paper.

Step 3. Measure and cut your stringing material

Make sure you have enough length of stringing material for your bracelet by measuring it and adding extra for knotting and fastening clasps. Make sure to use the proper tools to cut any cord, nylon thread, or beading wire to the right length.

Step 4. String the Beads

Now for the exciting part: threading the beads onto the material of your choice. Utilize your design as a reference and adhere to your intended pattern. For smaller beads, you can use beading needles, and a basic needle threader can help with the threading process.

Step 5: Tighten the Laces

Fasten the bracelet's ends once all the beads have been strung. To secure the beads, you can use clamshell bead tips, crimp beads, or knots, depending on the type of material you've chosen. Make sure there are no loose ends on the bracelet.

6. Include the Clasp

Put the clasp of your choice on both ends of the bracelet. If you are using a traditional clasp, you may need to use jump rings or crimp beads for this step. Connecting with a magnetic clasp is easier.

Step 7: Assess Fit

Make sure your bracelet fits properly on your wrist by checking its length and making any required adjustments before finishing it.

Step 8: Include the last details

Make sure all knots and clasps are secure and trim any extra stringing material to give your bracelet a professional appearance. If you'd like, you can also add charms or spacer beads.

Step 9: Examine Wear

Try on your freshly designed bracelet to ensure that it fits well and looks the way you had imagined. If necessary, adjustments can still be made at this point.

Step 10: Display Your Work

Best wishes! Your bracelet is now complete. It's now time to show off your artistry by giving it to someone special or wearing it with pride.

Making bracelets is a flexible craft that invites countless variations and expressions of creativity. As you get more skilled, you can play around with various bead kinds, patterns, and techniques to make one-of-a-kind creations that express your flair. You can make beautiful jewelry that you'll cherish for years to come by following this step-by-step tutorial, whether you're making bracelets for yourself or as gifts. Have fun creating!

CHAPTER THREE

Advanced Techniques On How To Make Bracelets

Bracelet making is a fun and well-liked craft that helps you express your creativity and make stunning wearable art. Although there are a lot of fundamental bracelet-making techniques, more sophisticated ones might help you become an even better bracelet maker.

We will go through advanced bracelet-making methods in this guide, such as wire wrapping, macramé, and bead weaving.

1. Macramé Necklaces:

• Square Knots: The fundamental technique in macramé is the square knot. If you combine square knots in different ways, you can make quite complex patterns.

• Half Hitch Knots: In macramé bracelets, half hitch knots are used to create diagonal designs.

• Micro Macramé: This technique creates delicate and detailed patterns by employing smaller cords and more complex knots.

2. Weaving beads:

• Peyote weave: Using this off-loom method of bead weaving, you may weave beads together to form intricate patterns that resemble bricks.

• Right Angle Weave: This method produces a flexible, textured bracelet by weaving beads into a grid pattern.

• Herringbone Stitch: This stitch is excellent for constructing bracelets with a thinner profile since it produces a V-shaped design.

3. Wrapping wires:

• Basic Wire Wrapping: Acquire the skill to manufacture wire-wrapped links to join gemstones and beads so you may build personalized designs.

• Spiral Wire Wrapping: This method adds an exquisite touch to your bracelets by using wire to form gorgeous spirals.

• Frame Wire Wrapping: To create a distinctive, eye-catching look, wireframes are created around stones or beads.

4. The Kumihimo

• Round Braid: Bracelets can be made using the Japanese braiding method known as Kumihimo. You can use a variety of color patterns to create beautiful round braids.

• Flat Braid: Try out various combinations of beads and thread to create wide, flat bracelets with elaborate patterns.

5. Resin Necklaces:

• Embedding Objects: To add a unique touch to your bracelet, use resin to embed little items like flowers, shells, or even miniature portraits.

• Layed Resin: You can add different textures and components to your bracelets by pouring resin in stages and creating multi-layered bracelets.

6. Metal Engraving:

• Metal Stamped Bracelets: Add personal touches to your metal bracelets by imprinting important messages, dates, or names on metal blanks. Apply patinas or enamel to the finish to create depth.

6. Composite Clay:

• Millefiori Technique: This technique uses polymer clay to create elaborate patterns that are then sliced to create vibrant beads for bracelets.

• Caning: Using layers and rolling clay, caning is a different method for creating intricate designs with polymer clay.

8. Expert-Level Beading:

- Soutache: To create gorgeous, three-dimensional bracelets, soutache entails sewing together complicated patterns with beads and crystals.

- Bead embroidery: Stitch beads onto leather or fabric to create bracelets with a textured, rich appearance.

9. Using Stones in Your Designs:

- Wire-wrapped gemstones: Bracelets with aesthetic appeal and therapeutic qualities can be created by combining wire wrapping with gemstones.

- Gemstone Loom Beading: Create elaborate bracelet designs with jewels by using a bead loom.

10. More Complex Knotting Methods:

- Celtic Knots: To create a beautiful and significant bracelet, learn how to weave complicated Celtic knots using leather or cords.

• Turk's Head Knots: You can use these beautiful, complicated knots as the centrepieces of your bracelets.

Gaining proficiency in these sophisticated bracelet-making methods can be a fulfilling and artistic experience. As you get better, you'll be able to create one-of-a-kind, customized bracelets that highlight your abilities and sense of style. Don't be scared to try new things, combine different methods, and develop your style when it comes to producing bracelets.

Customizing Your Bracelets

Creating one-of-a-kind bracelets that express your interests, style, and personality is a great way to give your accessories a personalized touch. You can use a variety of techniques and materials to customize your bracelets, depending on whether you want to create a statement piece with a striking, one-of-a-kind design or a subtle, exquisite piece. We'll go over all the details of customizing bracelets in this tutorial, including materials, processes, and design inspiration.

Step 1: Inspiration for Design

Getting ideas for your bracelet's design is crucial before you begin editing it.

Take inspiration from the following sources:

1. Personal Interests: Consider your passions, interests, and pastimes. If you're a nature lover, for instance, you might want to include flower or leaf themes in your design.

2. Styles and colors that are in right now are widely worn; keep an eye on these trends.

It is possible to modify these styles for your bracelet design.

3. Color Palette: Select a color scheme that goes well with your clothing and expresses your sense of style. To produce a design that is both harmonic and visually appealing, think about applying color theory.

4. Important Symbols: Use charms or symbols that are meaningful to you personally.

These could be birthstones, initials, or religious symbols.

5. Texture and Materials: To give your design more depth and variation, experiment with various textures and materials like leather, beads, crystals, or metals.

Step 2: Material Selection

One of the most important parts of personalizing your bracelet is selecting the materials.

These are a few typical items you could utilize:

First. Glass, wood, plastic, and gemstones are just a few of the materials and shapes that beads can be made with. Beads can be combined to make complex patterns.

2. Charms: You can personalize your bracelet by adding charms. From hearts and stars to animals and travel-themed motifs, they are available in an extensive variety of shapes and themes.

3. Wire: To provide structure and keep charms or beads together, use wire. For your design, you can select from a variety of wire gauges and colors.

4. Thread and Cord: You can string beads or make macramé patterns with thread and cord made of materials like nylon, silk, or leather.

5. Choose clasps and fasteners that complement the design and operation of your bracelet. Popular options include magnetic clasps, toggle clasps, and lobster clasps.

6. Tools: To put your bracelet together, you might need pliers, wire cutters, and bead needles, depending on your design.

Step 3: Types and Methods of Bracelets

There are many different kinds of bracelets and ways to personalize your jewelry:

1. String Bracelets: These bracelets are easy to wear and have many uses. You can use charms, beads, and knots to make patterns. For string

bracelets, macramé and friendship bracelet techniques are popular.

2. Beaded Bracelets: To make a beaded bracelet, thread beads onto a wire or string.

To create one-of-a-kind designs, play around with different bead sizes, shapes, and patterns.

Three. Small charms are fastened to a chain or bracelet base to create charm bracelets.

Over time, you can customize your charm bracelet by adding more significant charms.

4. Wristbands: Wristbands provide a broad, level surface for personalization. To make a standout piece, you can engrave metal cuffs or add embellishments like leather, fabric, or gemstones.

5. Wrap Bracelets: These bracelets consist of lengthy strands that round your wrist several times. They can be embellished with fabric, leather, or beads to give them a layered, textured appearance.

Step 4: Completing and Assembling

To construct and complete your bracelet, follow these steps after choosing your materials, the type of bracelet, and the finishing technique:

1. Measure: Establish the required bracelet length and cut the materials to that length.

2. Layout: Before assembling, lay out your design on a level surface.

This enables you to see the finished result and make any required changes.

3. Assembling: Begin putting your bracelet together using the selected method. Pay close attention to details, making sure that knots are tight and beads are positioned evenly.

4. closing: To ensure a safe closing, fasten each end of your bracelet with the selected clasp or fastener. Verify that it is simple to open and close.

5. Final Details: If required, polish the bracelet, tuck in loose ends, and trim away any excess material. Additionally, you can personalize it by

affixing a tiny tag bearing your initials or a heartfelt note.

Step 5: Upkeep and Care

Take note of these maintenance suggestions to make sure your personalized bracelet lasts a long time:

First. Avoid Water and Chemicals: Since water and chemicals might harm some materials, take off your bracelet before going swimming or using cleaning supplies.

2. Store Carefully: To avoid dust and scratches, keep your bracelet in a jewelry box or purse when not in use.

Three. Clean Gently: To maintain the best possible appearance for your bracelet, use a soft cloth or a jewelry cleaning solution made especially for the materials it is made of.

4. Examine Often: Keep an eye out for any loose clasps, charms, or beads, and fix any issues as soon as they arise.

Personalizing your bracelets is a fun and creative way to show off your sense of style and individuality. Beautiful, unique bracelets that you'll treasure for years to come can be designed and made with a little inspiration, the correct supplies, and a little perseverance.

So, start putting your creativity to use and start personalizing your bracelets right away!

Caring For Your Bracelets

Bracelets are more than just stylish accessories—they may be sentimental items with lasting value. Whether your collection consists of delicate bangles, hefty statement pieces, or sophisticated wristwatches, you must take good care of your bracelets to guarantee their continued beauty and functionality for many years to come. This is a comprehensive guide to bracelet maintenance:

First. Recognize Your Sources:

• Various bracelet materials need different maintenance. Materials that are frequently used include leather, beads, jewels, stainless steel, gold, and silver. The first step in taking care of your bracelet is to understand its makeup.

2. How to Clean Your Bracelets:

• To avoid general wear and tear, grime accumulation, and tarnishing, regular cleaning is essential.

• Gold and Silver: Gently wipe the surface using a delicate, lint-free cloth. Use a solution of water and mild dish soap or a moderate jewelry cleaner on tarnished parts.

• Stainless steel: scrub with a moist cloth and a small amount of soap, then rinse and completely dry.

• Leather: Keep it away from water since it can deteriorate it. To keep the leather supple and stop it from cracking, use a leather conditioner.

• Bracelets with beads and gemstones: Wipe with a gentle, moist cloth. Steer clear of harsh cleaners that can harm the gemstones or beads.

3. Holding:

• To avoid tangles and scratches, store your bracelets individually. To keep your jewelry secure and arranged, use compartmentalized organizers, jewelry boxes, or bags.

• To keep your gold and silver bracelets from tarnishing, use anti-tarnish pouches or strips in your storage containers.

4. Prevent Exposure:

• Chemicals can harm different types of materials, so keep your bracelets away from things like hairspray, lotions, perfumes, and home cleaners.

Take off wristbands before taking a bath, going swimming, or doing any other activity that can expose them to water or a lot of moisture.

5. Wear carefully:

• Take care when putting on your bracelets.

Do not tug or stretch them as this can cause the materials to deteriorate.

• If your bracelet has closures or clasps, make sure you securely fasten them to avoid breaking.

6. Expert Upkeep:

• Take your bracelets to a qualified jeweler regularly for upkeep and inspection. They can look for any problems that need to be fixed, such as loose stones or damaged clasps.

6. Guard Against Physical Injury:

• Use caution when playing sports or performing hard lifting or other physical activity that could cause an impact on your bracelets. Take them out to avoid harm.

8. Beads and Fragile Stones:

Pearls are especially fragile. Avert exposing them to heat, acids, or chemicals by storing them apart.

• Special attention may be needed for delicate gemstones such as opal and emeralds.

See a jeweler for advice relevant to your situation.

In 9. Examine Strapless Bracelets:

• Be mindful that bracelets with elastic cords may eventually wear out if you own any.

To avoid breaking them, check and restring them frequently.

10. Turn Your Jewels Around:

• To avoid overuse, switch up your bracelet every day. To extend the life of your jewelry and maintain excellent condition, rotate it.

Maintaining your bracelets will keep their aesthetic value intact as well as their emotional and monetary worth. Your bracelets can continue to be priceless and significant heirlooms that you can pass down to future generations if you give them the care they need. Always adhere to the care instructions related to the materials and design of your bracelets, keeping in mind that each one is unique.

Showcasing Your Bracelets Work

Promoting your jewelry business or just sharing your creative passion with a wider audience requires you to display your bracelet work.

Either as a jewelry maker for a living or as a pastime, showcasing your bracelets well can help you become known, draw clients, and improve your skills. This is a comprehensive instruction about how to present your bracelet designs:

First. Superior Photography:

To get crisp, detailed photos of your bracelets, use a high-resolution camera for your smartphone or a decent camera.

Use diffused artificial light or natural light to accentuate the colors and textures of your bracelets.

• To avoid unsteady photos, think about using a tripod or stabilizer.

• Try out different viewpoints and angles to get the most eye-catching pictures.

2. Establish a Specialized Workspace:

• Arrange your workplace so that it is clear of clutter and ready for bracelet photos. You may make your bracelets stand out with a background that is visually attractive or neutral.

Organize your bracelets for photos on a table or in a jewelry display.

Three. Using Styling and Props:

• Add accessories to your bracelet, like seashells, fresh flowers, or pretty stones, to match its style.

A lifestyle element, such as hands, wrists, or model images, might be used to highlight how the bracelet appears on the wearer.

• Watch that the props don't take attention away from your bracelet, which is the major attraction.

4. Relentless Branding:

• Create a recognizable brand and style for your jewelry photography. This involves adding a watermark with your brand, filters, and a particular color scheme.

• Professionalism and recognition are fostered by consistency in brand identification.

5. Take Close-Ups and Detailed Pictures:

To highlight the fine details on your bracelets, take close-up pictures.

• Draw attention to special details like beadwork, charms, and clasps.

6. Retouch and edit images:

Utilize software for photo editing to improve your pictures. To bring the colors of the bracelet to life, adjust brightness, contrast, and color balance.

• Eliminate any flaws or dust accumulations that could detract from your jewelry.

6. Create an Online Identity:

• Use websites to display your bracelets or use social media sites like Facebook, Instagram, or Etsy.

• Make sure your website is responsive to mobile devices and easy to use.

• Craft engrossing product descriptions that narrate the history of each bracelet's components.

8. Activate Your Viewers:

• Engage with your audience by swiftly answering messages and comments from followers and potential clients.

Establish a personal connection with your audience by sharing your creative process, behind-the-scenes experiences, and sources of inspiration.

In 9. Network and Cooperate:

• To cross-promote your work and attract a larger audience, collaborate with other jewelry makers or artists.

• Attend art exhibits, jewelry exhibits, or craft fairs in your community to connect with other artists and possible clients.

Ten. Uphold Your Portfolio:

• Compile your greatest bracelet designs into a tangible or digital portfolio to present at conferences, trade shows, or when interacting with possible merchants.

• Update your portfolio frequently with fresh layouts and top-notch photos.

11. Request Input and Improvement:

• Don't be afraid to get opinions from friends, family, and clients.

• Always hone your photographic techniques and adjust to the ever-evolving jewelry presenting trends.

Twelve. Presentation and Packaging:

• Examine the way your bracelets are packaged. The experience of the consumer can be improved by a beautifully presented bracelet in a lovely box or pouch.

Keep in mind that showing off your bracelet creations is a continuous process. You should see an increase in the visibility and desirability of your work as you hone your photographic techniques and establish your brand.

In the cutthroat field of jewelry creation, persistence, innovation, and patience are keys to staying ahead of the competition.

CHAPTER FOUR

Inspiration And Resources: The Keys To Creativity And Success

Success and creativity frequently go hand in hand and both rely significantly on two fundamental pillars: resources and inspiration. These factors are crucial in determining the course of your journey, regardless of your profession—artist, scientist, entrepreneur, or anybody else aiming to accomplish their objectives. We'll go deep into the importance of resources and inspiration, their interactions, and how to use them to your advantage in this investigation.

The Inspirational Power

1. Putting Fuel on the Creative Fire: The spark that starts the creative process is inspiration. It's the spark of inspiration when your mind makes connections between seemingly unconnected concepts, opening doors to creativity. Without inspiration, coming up with creative ideas becomes difficult, and reaching greatness can seem unachievable.

2. Diverse Sources: There are many different places to find inspiration. It could come from the wonders of nature, an engrossing book, an intellectual discussion, or even a personal experience. It's important to maintain an open mind and be open to ideas coming from unexpected places.

3. Personal Transformation: You can change your life through inspiration. Something that strikes a deep chord with you has the power to change your outlook, objectives, and even your purpose. Deep inspiration has given birth to many notable technologies and artistic creations.

4. Developing Inspiration: Although it frequently happens suddenly, there are strategies to develop inspiration.

Take part in mentally stimulating activities, like traveling, reading, or experiencing other cultures. Assemble a broad network of thought partners and ideas around you to foster an ongoing stream of inspiration.

The Function Of Materials

First. Realizing Dreams: Resources are useful tools that enable you to realize the thoughts that have inspired you. Resources—whether they be in the form of money, time, tools, or knowledge—are what stand between creativity and success.

2. Resources are an investment in your growth and your objectives. They make it possible for you to create a prototype, finance research, or learn new skills. Your innovative ideas could stay pipe dreams if you lack the necessary finances.

Three. possibilities to expedite Your trip: Resources frequently offer possibilities to expedite your trip. Financial resources, for example, can be used to hire talented staff or attend educational programs. Access to networking resources can lead to partnerships and collaborations.

4. Being resourceful: It's crucial to remember that being resourceful, or knowing how to maximize the resources at hand, can be just as significant as having a lot of them. Because they push you to think outside the box, situations with limited resources are typically conducive to creativity and invention.

The Point Where Resources and Inspiration Collide

1. Synergy: When resources and inspiration come together, amazing things can happen. Encouraged concepts receive the backing they need to grow, and resources are directed toward worthwhile projects.

Beautiful artwork, ground-breaking discoveries, and prosperous enterprises can result from this combination.

2. Sustainability: Any endeavor's ability to succeed over the long term frequently depends on how well resources and inspiration are balanced. While having a lot of resources without inspiration might lead to pointless activities, having too much inspiration without the essential resources can lead to frustration.

3. Adaptability: The capacity to change course when faced with unforeseen events is essential. A lack of resources can occasionally spark fresh, more creative ideas, but an abundance of resources can allow you to change course when an inspired concept doesn't work out.

Creating Inspiration and Obtaining Materials

First. Never Stop Learning: Always be learning new things. Read widely, investigate novel subjects, and pursue lifelong learning.

This not only fosters creativity but also improves your capacity to obtain and apply resources efficiently.

2. Networking: Create a network of varied people who can offer resources, inspiration, and advice. Success can be shared when like-minded and complimentary thinkers collaborate.

Three. Create a financial plan that is in line with your objectives. Use resources carefully, put aside money for creativity and taking chances, and look for funding or investment options as necessary.

4. Resilience: Acknowledge that there may be many obstacles in the way of achievement. Remain strong in the face of adversity and seize the chance to improve your resource allocation and creative thinking.

In conclusion, the two most important components of every creative or fruitful journey are inspiration and resources.

Together, they enhance one another and help bring concepts to life. The secret to reaching your objectives and making a lasting impression on the world is having the capacity to successfully manage resources and inspire others. To reach your greatest potential, cultivate both creativity and resourcefulness and have an open mind to inspiration.

Conclusion

creating bracelets is more than simply a craft; it's a journey of connection, creativity, and self-expression. As we've looked at the delights of bracelet-making, it's clear that this straightforward yet meaningful hobby can capture people's hearts, promote mindfulness, and strengthen interpersonal relationships.

We may connect with our inner artists while crafting these little, detailed pieces of jewelry, which offer a relaxing diversion from the stress of everyday life.

We can express our ideas, feelings, and uniqueness via the process of choosing beads, patterns, and colors. Every bracelet turns into a blank canvas that we can fill with our aspirations, goals, and desires. It's a journey of self-discovery as we investigate our aesthetic tastes, uncover the beauty in flaws, and develop the patience needed for laborious tasks.

The joy of creating bracelets is age-, gender-, and background-neutral. This art form appeals to all ages, whether you are a youngster making friendship bracelets at summer camp, an adolescent designing a fashionable accessory, an adult looking for a calming activity, or a senior remembering simpler times. It's a common tongue that spans generations and makes it possible to share experiences, knowledge, and emotions.

Moreover, for individuals who want to convert their hobby into a business, bracelet creation has the potential to be a fulfilling and even lucrative endeavor. The need for distinctive and customized jewelry keeps driving the growth of the handmade jewelry market. Using this craft as a launching pad into the enterprise will allow you to show off your artistic abilities and creative vision to a wider audience.

It's crucial to keep in mind that the process is just as worthwhile as the final product as we come to the end of our investigation of the delights of bracelet manufacturing. The experience includes the fulfillment of making something lovely by hand, the delight of giving a personalized bracelet to a special someone, and the sense of achievement that arises from learning new skills.

In your subsequent attempts at making bracelets, keep exploring and trying new things. There are a gazillion patterns, methods, and supplies all waiting for you to explore.

Accept that learning is a process, and don't be scared to make mistakes—they frequently result in lovely, unexpected outcomes. Look to nature, art, and culture for inspiration to give your work a distinct personality.

Never forget that perfection comes from practice. Your talents will get more refined the more time you spend on the craft.

If you're interested in learning from seasoned craftsmen and connecting with other bracelet enthusiasts, think about enrolling in classes or joining crafting clubs. These exchanges can serve as a source of companionship, encouragement, and inspiration.

Finally, spread the word to others about your love of producing bracelets.

Teach this ageless art form to your friends, family, and kids. You will not only impart a useful skill but also generate enduring memories and fortify your relationships.

In conclusion, creating bracelets is an artistic endeavor that enriches our lives and fosters creativity, joy, and connection. It is much more than just a pastime. So, gather your tools, beads, and strings and set out on a voyage of self-discovery and self-expression. The world of bracelet making is a lovely one, ready for you to discover and enjoy, whether you're making them for yourself, giving them to special people, or even turning your hobby into a company.

THE END

Printed in Great Britain
by Amazon

42388986R00046